THE STRIPLING
WARRIOR AND WARRIORETTE
WORKOUT

THE STRIPLING WARRIOR AND WARRIORETTE WORKOUT

EXERCISES TO INCREASE YOUR SPIRITUAL STRENGTH

SHANE BARKER

DESERET
BOOK

SALT LAKE CITY, UTAH

For Josh, Spencer, Devin, and Hunter

Library of Congress Cataloging-in-Publication Data

Barker, Shane R.
    The stripling warrior and warriorette workout / Shane Barker.
        p.   cm.
    ISBN 978-1-59038-927-0 (paperbound)
    1. Mormon youth—Religious life.   2. Mormon youth—Conduct of life.
I. Title.
    BX8643.Y6B36 2008
    248.8'30882893—dc22   2008012444

Printed in the United States of America
Sheridan Books, Chelsea, MI

10   9   8   7   6   5   4   3   2   1

Contents

CONTENTS

FOREWORD

Helaman's stripling warriors.

Wow!

Those fantastic young men have always been among my favorite Book of Mormon heroes. The word *stripling* means they were "mere youths." Today we might say they were "just kids."

But those "kids" went up against an army of older, more experienced Lamanite warriors. And according to Helaman, "They . . . fought as if with the strength of God; . . . and with such mighty power did they fall upon the Lamanites, that they did frighten them; and for this cause did the Lamanites deliver themselves up as prisoners of war" (Alma 56:56).

"Imagine that!" Elder M. Russell Ballard once said. "These inexperienced young men were so spiritually and physically prepared, and so powerful, that they frightened their foes into surrendering!" ("The Greatest Generation of Missionaries," *Ensign,* Nov. 2002, 46).

I get chills just thinking about it!

And the question I've always had is *How did they get that way?*

I'm sure that Helaman gave his young warriors drills that honed and sharpened their fighting skills. But I believe they had *spiritual* workouts, too. I believe they had activities and exercises that built their spiritual muscles so that they were ready when God needed them most.

Today we are facing battles that are every bit as challenging as those faced by Helaman's stripling warriors. And once again the Lord needs valiant young men and women who have the courage to stand up for what they believe in.

I'm not just talking about your seminary president or the Laurel counselor in the next ward.

I'm talking about *you!*

You see, in the premortal world you decided to follow the Savior when you were truly put to the test. And now the Lord needs you to strap on your armor and do it again. He needs you to stand up for what's right and live up to your standards as valiantly as you did then. And he needs you to start *now!*

How do you do that? Well, that's what *The Stripling Warrior—and Warriorette—Workout* is all about. It's about building your spiritual muscles. It's about becoming an extraordinary teenager—a *valiant* teenager—who's ready to stand up for what's right. It's about becoming a latter-day stripling warrior who's ready when the Lord needs you.

Are you ready?

Great!

Let's get started!

1

CRASHING ON A MOUNTAIN BIKE!

Being a Valiant Teenager

Jake Allen shot down the trail on his mountain bike, flying over a bump and skidding to a stop.

"Shane!" he yelled, dropping his bike and running across the grass. "Shane! Riley's been hurt! You've got to come fast!"

I dropped my shovel and grabbed Jake by the shoulders. "What's wrong? What happened?"

The thirteen-year-old boy was so out of breath that it took several seconds before he could speak clearly.

"It's Riley," he repeated. "He crashed . . . on his bike. He's hurt bad."

"Okay," I said. "Slow down and tell me exactly what happened."

Jake took a deep breath and quickly told me the story. It was Saturday, and we were high in the mountains at the Boy Scout camp where we both worked. I was spending the day catching up on some repairs while Jake and his friends rode their mountain bikes to a nearby lake. They had stopped by to visit a short time earlier, and then continued on down the mountain.

"Riley was going really fast," Jake said. "He got ahead of us and wiped out. When we found him, he was crumpled up in the middle of the trail. His head's bleeding and he says his back hurts. We think something might be broken."

"Where is he now?"

Jake pointed. "On the trail. About two miles away."

"Okay," I said. "Let's go."

We threw Jake's bike into the back of my truck and drove as far as we could on the mountain road; then we raced on down the trail, me on foot and Jake bumping along on his bike. When we found Riley, the boy was flat on his back, moaning softly. The rest of his friends were gathered around him, wide-eyed and frightened.

"Hey, Riley," I said, kneeling beside the injured boy. "How're you feeling?"

"Bad," he said. "My back hurts."

"Where does it hurt?" I asked. "Is it worse by your hips or up by your shoulders?"

"My hips."

I nodded. Someone had wrapped a bandana around Riley's head. It was soaked with blood, though the bleeding seemed to have stopped. And his back . . . I knew that back injuries could be serious. We couldn't move him without possibly making things even worse.

We were going to need more help.

"Okay, Riley," I said. "I want you to stay completely still. *Don't move!* Do you understand me?"

"Yes."

"Okay, then. I'll be right back."

I looked up at the group of boys surrounding us. They all knew their friend was in bad shape, and they were scared. And a couple of them were now going to have to go down the mountain for help. The boys were all dependable. But with Riley's life in danger, there was no question about whom I was going to send.

"Jake," I said, standing and motioning for him to follow me. "Come here."

I took Jake a short distance away and said: "I'm not sure how bad Riley's hurt. But we can't take any chances. I need you to ride down the canyon and find a phone. Call 911. Tell them that Riley has a back injury and maybe a concussion. They'll probably need a search-and-rescue team to get him out of here. You'll need to meet the rescuers at the road and lead them back here. Can you do that?"

Jake nodded vigorously.

I put my hands on his shoulders and looked him in the eyes. "Are you sure you know what to do?"

He nodded confidently. "Yes," he said. "I can do it. Trust me."

"All right, then. Take Mike with you and *be careful!* Don't get hurt on the way, or we'll be in more trouble than we are now."

Jake and Mike took their bikes and shot down the trail.

Inside, I felt a sense of calm. The situation was serious, but I trusted Jake. I had known him for only a couple of months, but he was one of the finest young men I had ever known. He was trustworthy and dependable. I knew he would get the job done.

And he did. It turned out that Riley had a concussion and a broken pelvis and had to be airlifted off the mountain. But Jake had calmly and accurately described the situation to the sheriff's dispatcher and then guided the rescue team up the mountain and straight to his injured friend.

Sheriff's deputies said that Jake saved his friend's life.

Since then I've sometimes wondered—if our roles had been reversed—whether Jake would have sent *me*. I've wondered if I have earned the trust of those *I* serve.

Now, your Heavenly Father has important missions for *you,* too. When he does—when he has some crucial errand and needs a young man or a young woman to carry it out—can he count on you? Can he depend on you to get the job done?

Are you living your life so that he would consider sending you?

My friend Carly used to coach a basketball team. One night they were playing the best team in the league and were playing their best game ever. With less than a minute left they were behind by a single point.

And they had the ball.

"Erika!" Carly yelled to her point guard. "Time out! Call time out!"

Erika frantically gestured at the officials.

Carly stood looking at the scoreboard as her team huddled around. She had a tough decision to make. She had a play designed for this exact situation. She knew that with it she could win this game and beat the best team in the league. But she also knew that every player would have to execute. There was no room for mistakes. *Every player* would have to do her job exactly right.

She agonized for a moment, and then said, "Alissa, . . . go in for Susan."

The girls gaped in surprise. Susan was one of their best players. She was their tallest player, their best rebounder, and their best shooter.

But she wasn't disciplined.

More than anything, Carly wanted to keep Susan in the game. But she knew from past experience that Susan wouldn't run the play. Once she touched the ball she'd ignore everyone else and try to win the game all by herself. In other games, in similar situations, she'd taken the ball, dribbled around for a couple of seconds, and then taken the shot.

Carly knew that she would do the same thing tonight.

And Carly couldn't let her.

And so, with an important game on the line, Susan sat on the bench while someone else took her spot running the coach's play and winning the game.

Now, we live in a time when the forces of evil are more powerful than they have ever been. We live in a time when our Heavenly Father needs valiant young heroes more than ever before. He needs latter-day warriors—and warriorettes—like never before. At this critical time—with time running off the clock—who did he send into the game?

He sent *you!*

With so much hanging in the balance, who did he know he could count on?

You!

You see, in the premortal world you were *valiant*. You went the extra mile. In the battle for righteousness you did more than stand on the sidelines and cheer. You put on your armor and stood side-by-side with Jesus.

You proved yourself.

And now your Heavenly Father needs you again. He needs young people who do more than sit on the back row, half-heartedly living the gospel. He needs young people he can count on to set an example, live righteously, and show the way.

Like I counted on Jake, can He count on you to get the job done?

Or, like Susan, do you sit on the sidelines while the Lord sends someone else?

President Ezra Taft Benson once said: "You have

been born at this time for a sacred and glorious purpose. It is not by chance that you have been reserved to come to earth in this last dispensation of the fulness of times. Your birth at this particular time was foreordained in the eternities. You are the royal army of the Lord in the last days. You are 'youth of the noble birthright.' (*Hymns,* 1985, no. 255.) In the spiritual battles you are waging, I see you as today's sons [and daughters] of Helaman" ("To the Youth of the Noble Birthright," *Ensign,* May 1986, 43).

Bishop H. Burke Peterson echoed those thoughts: "My dear friends," he said, "you are a royal generation. You were preserved to come to the earth in this time for a special purpose. Not just a few of you, but all of you. There are things for each of you to do that no one else can do as well as you. If you do not prepare to do them, they will not be done. Your mission is unique and distinctive for you. Please don't make another have to take your place. He or she can't do it as well as you can. If you will let him, I testify that our Father in Heaven will walk with you through the journey of life and inspire you to know your special purpose here" ("Your Life Has a Purpose," *New Era,* May 1979, 4).

Make no mistake: you are here on this earth at this time because you proved that you were valiant.

Keep it up!

Keep going!

Remember that your Heavenly Father needs you. Your family and friends need you. They need young people who are doing their very best to set an example for them.

And that's what this book is about. It's about taking the talents and abilities the Lord has given you and developing them to their fullest. It's about preparing and proving yourself so that when the Lord needs you, you'll be ready. It's about standing tall and, like one of Helaman's stripling warriors, going into battle.

Are you ready?

Then start now! Begin preparing yourself so that when your turn comes the Lord can say, "I'll send *you!*"

WARRIOR WORKOUT TIPS

- Decide now that *you* will be a valiant teenager. Don't be satisfied thinking that being valiant is just something you *could* be. Don't be satisfied thinking that it's something you *should* be. Decide that being a valiant teenager—being a latter-day stripling warrior—is something that you absolutely, positively, 100 percent *will* be!

- Remember that *you* are here for a reason. Be sure that you are keeping yourself worthy for whatever the Lord has in store for you. Prepare now to be ready whenever the Lord needs you.

- Look for ways to begin serving your Father in Heaven. Participate in seminary, Young Women, and priesthood meetings. Be a good example to your friends. Look for people you can bless with an act of service, a kind word, or a friendly smile.

- Don't wait to get started! As the words of the hymn ask, "Who's on the Lord's side? Who? *Now* is the time to show" (*Hymns,* no. 260; emphasis added).

2

VALIANT TEENAGERS AND THE SONS OF LEHI

Becoming Valiant

"Valiant."

Brother Sanders, my tenth-grade seminary teacher, rubbed his chin and lifted an eyebrow.

"I need your help," he said, looking around the room. "The other day a student asked me what it means to be valiant, and I wasn't certain how to answer her. Does anyone have any ideas?"

"It means you're courageous," someone piped up.

"Courageous?"

"Yeah!" a second student replied. "And pure."

"Christlike," someone else added.

"And brave . . ."

After a moment, we began to see our teacher's point. Most of us knew what it meant to be valiant, but it wasn't an easy idea to put into words.

Brother Sanders listened to our definitions for another moment, and then shook his head. "I'm still not getting it," he said. "So let's try coming at it from a different angle. Let's make a list of people who we know are, or were, valiant."

Well, we thought, *this had to be easier . . .*

"Joseph Smith," someone said right away.

Brother Sanders wrote "Joseph Smith" on the chalkboard.

"President Kimball," someone else added, mentioning our newly sustained prophet.

"Moroni."

"Alma."

"*Alma,*" Brother Sanders said. He started to write, and then stopped. "Which Alma?" he asked, turning to look at the class.

"Both of them!"

Brother Sanders appeared puzzled. "But didn't Alma the Younger *persecute* people?" he asked. "Didn't he try to *destroy* the Church?"

"Not always," a young woman named Emily said. "He repented."

"Oh! So a person who's not valiant to begin with can change?"

"Of course!"

"Well, good!" Brother Sanders said. "*That* certainly makes me feel better. Now, who else can we put on the list?"

"Nephi," a young man named Brandon said in a let's-not-forget-the-obvious tone of voice.

Brother Sanders wrote "Nephi" on the board, but then quickly added "Laman" and "Lemuel."

"Hey!" a student named Mari said. "What are you doing?"

Brother Sanders tried to appear innocent.

"What?" he asked. "What's wrong?"

Mari pointed at the board with her best Hello!-What-do-you-think-you're-doing? expression. "Laman and Lemuel?" she asked. "*Puh-lease!* They weren't valiant!"

"But of course they were!"

There were several shouts of protest until Brother Sanders held up his hands to calm everyone down.

"Think about it," he said. "Laman and Lemuel were every bit as valiant as Nephi."

"*What?*" the class chorused.

"Well, didn't they go into the wilderness when Lehi asked them to?"

"Yes . . ."

"And didn't they help Nephi to get the plates of brass?"

"Yeah . . ."

"And didn't they help Nephi to build his ship?"

"Yes, but . . ."

Brother Sanders spread his hands. "Then why do you think they weren't valiant?"

A friend of mine named Lexi stood up with her hands on her hips. "Because they had *bad attitudes!*"

"Okay," Brother Sanders said, laughing. "Maybe we ought to change our list so that it looks like this . . ."

He turned to the board and drew a horizontal line, writing "Laman" and "Lemuel" on one end, and "Nephi" and "Moroni" on the other end so that it looked like this:

Nephi/Moroni ————————————Laman/Lemuel

"You know," he said, "being valiant is not always a cut-and-dried thing. For instance, if I asked you to show me where *you* are on the line, how many of you would place yourselves all the way over here with Nephi and Moroni?"

No one raised their hand.

"But I believe that *all* of you are valiant," he said. "Why? Because you're good. Because you're prayerful. Because you have faith and because you have strong testimonies." He tapped Nephi's end of the line. "And because you're all doing the *best you can* to get here."

Like everyone else in the room, I was beginning to understand. For the first time I was beginning to realize that even if I wasn't exactly like Nephi, I could still be valiant.

And it's true. You see, being valiant—especially as a teenager—doesn't mean that you have to be the ward Relief Society president. It doesn't mean that you have to be president of your seminary class. It doesn't mean that you have to be the first missionary in your group to become zone leader.

Instead, being valiant means doing the *best you can* to live the gospel. It means doing the best *you* can to serve your Heavenly Father. It means setting goals for yourself and then quietly and consistently striving to reach them.

It means doing the best you can to move yourself down the line.

I know a young woman named Ashley who's a

talented cellist. Even though she's only in the eighth grade, she plays better than many musicians many times her age. Even so, she practices hard every day, learning new pieces, taking private lessons, and constantly improving her technique.

Being valiant is like that. It's not like one day receiving a call from the bishop and hearing him say: "Congratulations! You've just passed the last requirement. You have just become valiant."

Instead, like Ashley improving at the cello, it's a daily, lifelong process. It means hanging in there during the easy times and in the hard times. It means getting up every day and doing your best to live the gospel and serve the Lord.

Are you still confused?

Then here are a couple of ideas to help you get started.

BE LIKE CHRIST

As you strive to be valiant, there are many examples you can follow. Prophets from the Book of Mormon, for instance. Joseph Smith and President Thomas S. Monson. Your parents or your ward or seminary leaders. Young people you know from school.

But the best example is the Savior himself.

Remember that Jesus was once your age. The exact age you are now! Life was different then, but he still faced many of the same challenges that you do. How do you suppose he handled them? And how do you suppose he would handle the problems *you* face?

Imagine for a moment that Jesus were living his teenage years today. And imagine that you were one of his friends. What sort of things do you think you'd do together? Tease or make fun of other kids at school? Watch suggestive movies? Listen to vulgar music or play violent video games?

Of course, you wouldn't!

We say it so often that sometimes it loses its meaning. But when you face a hard choice, ask yourself, *What* would *Jesus do?* Then really think about it. It's not just a cute little saying. Deciding how Jesus might handle a problem that you face might give you the proper perspective as you search for a solution. And if you let that thought guide your decisions, you'll never be wrong.

And here's another thing: we don't know a lot about the Lord's teenage years. Luke simply records that,

"Jesus increased in wisdom and stature, and *in favour with God and man*" (Luke 2:52; emphasis added).

Did you catch that? *In favor with God and man.*

I believe that means that Jesus was respected. It means he was liked. In modern terms, you might say he was popular. What does that mean to you? I think it means that you can live the gospel and still be accepted by your peers. You can be clean and pure and still be popular among your friends.

I have a young friend named Nick who used to play on my baseball team. One day when he was hanging out with a group of friends the conversation became ugly and offensive. Without a word, Nick walked away. He didn't cause a fuss. He didn't create any excitement. He didn't make any accusations.

He simply left.

A moment later a boy named Sam left, too. When Sam caught up with Nick, he said, "Thanks for leaving. I wanted to go, too, but I felt too embarrassed to leave until you did."

Nick just shrugged and wiggled his fingers: he was wearing a CTR ring.

"When things like that happen," he said, "I just choose the right."

There's no question that teenagers today face tough challenges. But when you come up against temptations, follow the example of the Savior. Try to be like him. Like we used to sing in Primary, "Try, try, try!" ("Jesus Once Was a Little Child," *Children's Songbook,* 55).

SEEK THE INFLUENCE OF THE HOLY GHOST

As you follow the example of the Savior, the Holy Ghost will help you to make good decisions. But he can do more than that. The Holy Ghost can also help you to *resist* temptations. When you enjoy the companionship of the Holy Ghost, many temptations will even stop tempting you.

Whoa!

Is that true?

Absolutely! President Spencer W. Kimball once wrote, "If heeded, [the Holy Ghost] will guide, inspire, and warn, and will *neutralize* the promptings of the evil one" (*The Miracle of Forgiveness* [Salt Lake City: Bookcraft, 1969] 14; emphasis added).

That means that when the Holy Ghost is with you, telling an off-color joke is something that doesn't occur to you. Watching an inappropriate movie is something that doesn't seem appealing to you. Breaking the Word of Wisdom is something that doesn't interest you.

I once took a group of young people from my ward to the Provo Temple to be baptized for the dead. It was a wonderful, marvelous, deeply spiritual experience.

Afterwards, as we returned to the bishop's home for ice cream, I was amazed at how different everyone seemed. They were all good kids. But that night they were even more so. They had just enjoyed a touching, moving experience and they were acting accordingly. Do you think anyone was fighting over who got to sit in the front seat?

They weren't.

Do you think anyone was telling inappropriate jokes or stories?

They weren't.

Do you think there was a lot of teasing and rough-housing in the car?

No, there wasn't.

Having the companionship of the Holy Ghost will have the same effect on you. It will help to weaken and even *neutralize* those temptations that trouble you. It will help you to become more like your Heavenly Father.

Remember that when you were baptized, you were directed to *receive* the Holy Ghost. It was not told to go to you; *you* were told to *receive* it.

So do it! Live your life so that the Holy Ghost can guide and inspire you. Keep yourself worthy so that the Holy Ghost becomes your *constant* companion.

"*Now is the time* to organize and prepare ourselves to have the Holy Ghost as our constant companion," Elder Robert D. Hales said. "This means doing what your parents and leaders have taught you to do—study the scriptures; pray morning and night; keep a neat, well-groomed appearance; follow a schedule; set and achieve goals; be honest in your dealings; keep commitments. . . . Always, always live the standards, revealed by the prophets, in the booklet *For the Strength of Youth*" ("To the Aaronic Priesthood: Preparing for the Decade of Decision," *Ensign*, May 2007, 49; emphasis added).

"When we understand . . . the gift of the Holy Ghost, it will change our lives," Elder Hales also said. "When temptations come our way, if we will listen, the Holy Ghost will remind us that we have promised to remember our Savior and obey the commandments of God" ("The Covenant of Baptism: To Be in the Kingdom and of the Kingdom," *Ensign*, Nov. 2000, 7).

When you keep yourself worthy of the influence of the Holy Ghost, living the gospel is easier. Resisting temptations is easier. Being valiant is easier.

PRAY ALWAYS

If you want to be valiant, it's probably because you love your Father in Heaven and want to become like him. You want to become closer to him. And one of the best ways to do that is to pray.

"There is no other resource to compare with prayer," President Gordon B. Hinckley once said. "To think that each of us may approach our Father in Heaven, who is the great God of the universe, for individual help and guidance, for strength and faith, is a miracle in and of itself" ("Great Shall Be the Peace of Thy Children," *Ensign,* Nov. 2000, 50).

Yes, you can become closer to your Heavenly Father through prayer—but your prayers must be sincere.

I was once on a cross-country ski trip when we were hit by an avalanche. Seven people were swept away in the snow. Three of them were completely buried and—unable to breathe beneath the snow—were soon unconscious. By an absolute miracle we found everyone before they suffocated, and we soon had everyone dug out of the snow.

But there was another problem. We were still stranded on the mountain. The seven victims were wet and cold. Hypothermia was setting in.

We needed help, and we needed it fast.

I skied off the mountain like a rocket. My job was to get to a truck, drive to a nearby ski resort, and phone for help.

Just seconds after I began to drive, though, the truck began making funny sounds. The engine clanked. There didn't seem to be any power.

Oh, no, I thought. *Not now . . . please, not now!*

Stomping my foot on the gas pedal, trying to force the truck up the mountain, I began to pray. I mean, I *really* began to pray! Lives depended on my getting to a telephone, and I couldn't afford mechanical problems now. I prayed harder than I ever had in my life.

There have probably been times when you've prayed that hard, too. Maybe even harder.

And there may have been times when you've simply said "habit" prayers. You know the kind: prayers that you say mechanically without really thinking about what you're saying.

But if you want to develop a serious relationship with your Heavenly Father, pray sincerely. Pray often. And pray with meaning. Open your heart and *talk* to him. Talk to him as if he's really there, and as if he's really listening. Because you know what? He really is!

As you follow the example of Jesus, seek the influence of the Holy Ghost, and become closer to your Heavenly Father through prayer, many other things will fall into place. You'll find yourself moving faster and faster toward Nephi's side of the valiant line. You'll find that with this start you can become as valiant as any of your scriptural heroes. You'll become more and more like Helaman's army, and you will *be* a modern stripling warrior!

WARRIOR WORKOUT TIPS

- Remember to be like Christ. Follow his example. Whenever you face tough choices, remember to ask yourself, "What would Jesus do?"

- Seek the influence and companionship of the Holy Ghost in all you do. Keep yourself worthy of its promptings and follow them when they come.

- Pray often. And pray with meaning. Open your heart and really *talk* with your Heavenly Father.
- Remember the valiant line. Be sure that you're doing your best—your very best—to keep yourself moving toward Nephi's end of the line.

3

CAMPING, SKIING, AND MEETING MISS WASATCH

Keeping Yourself Clean

Brady Glenn grinned through a face smudged with dirt.

"You know the first thing I'm gonna do when I get home?"

I could guess, but I asked anyway. "What's that?"

"I'm gonna take a shower," he said. "Then I'm gonna sit in the bathtub for an hour. And *then* I'm gonna take another shower."

I laughed. "You think that's going to be enough to get you clean again?"

"No," Brady said, shaking his head. "But it'll feel *real* good!"

I laughed again. Brady and I were on our way home from a three-day survival trip. For the past three days we'd hiked and camped in the desert of southern Utah, eating weird things and sleeping in the dirt. Even now Brady's hair was suspended in mid-explosion, filled with sand and tiny bits of sagebrush.

I looked pretty much the same. I was certain that two showers and an hour in the bathtub wouldn't even *begin* to get me feeling clean again.

But we'd had a great time. As I drove onto the street leading to Brady's home we were both feeling fantastic.

"Hey!" Brady said as we neared his home. "Look— Miss Wasatch is here! You finally get to say hi!"

I recoiled in horror. "Miss Wasatch" was Brady's older sister, Debbie. Brady had been wanting to introduce us for weeks, and I was excited to meet her. Debbie had been a cheerleader in high school and had recently won the Miss Wasatch Scholarship Pageant. Like little brothers everywhere, Brady enjoyed teasing her, often referring to her as "Miss Wasatch," or the "little cheerleader."

And now he was practically bouncing in his seat. "Finally!" he said. "You're both here at the same time! C'mon in so I can introduce you!"

"Are you *crazy?*" I asked. "There's no way I'm gonna meet her looking like this!"

"Oh, don't worry 'bout it," he said, looking me up and down. "You look fine. You just don't smell so good."

"Thanks," I said, shaking my head. "But no way! I'm not going anywhere *near* your sister until I've had a chance to clean up."

And I meant it. When Brady's parents finally invited me over for dinner one night so that I could meet Debbie, I put on my best clothes and made sure that I looked my very best.

Wouldn't you?

I remember another time when I was in high school. I was going to apply for a job at the local mall. It was a job that I really wanted, and I needed to make the best impression I could. When I went for my interview, I made sure I was wearing my very best clothes and looking as good as I possibly could.

Wouldn't you?

Of course, you would!

Now imagine that you were invited to an interview with your stake president, the prophet, or even the Savior himself. Wouldn't you want to look your best? Wouldn't you want your clothes to be nice and fresh and clean? Wouldn't you want to brush your teeth and check to be certain that your hair was just right?

More important, wouldn't you want to be fresh and clean on the *inside,* too?

Of course, you would! You'd want to be free of the stains and burdens of sins and mistakes. You'd want to be *worthy* to be in the presence of your leaders or Savior.

Now here's a great truth: valiant teenagers don't wait until they have an interview with the bishop to clean themselves up. They don't wait until they need their Heavenly Father's help before making themselves worthy.

They keep themselves clean, ready, and worthy *all the time!*

I'm a schoolteacher. And at the end of every term I have students come in to discuss their grades. Some of them say things like, "I know I've slacked off this term. But if you'll raise my grade I promise I'll do better next term."

Unfortunately, some young people approach their Heavenly Father the same way. When they need help or a blessing of some kind, they pray and say, "I know I haven't been doing my part. But help me now, and I promise I'll start doing better."

Not a good strategy!

It's so much better—it's so much more effective—

when you can kneel humbly in prayer and say: "Heavenly Father, you know how hard I'm trying. You know I'm trying to be good. You *know* I'm doing my best. Please help me now!"

When you keep yourself worthy of your Heavenly Father's blessings, your confidence can "wax strong in the presence of God," and the Holy Ghost can be your constant companion (see D&C 121:45–46).

The Psalmist wrote: "Who shall ascend into the hill of the Lord? or who shall stand in his holy place? He that hath *clean hands* and a *pure heart*" (Psalm 24:3–4; emphasis added).

Keeping yourself free of the burdens of sins and mistakes is what the Psalmist meant by having clean hands. And that's what this chapter is about.

How do you get started?

Let's take a look.

RECOGNIZE WHEN YOU'RE DOING WRONG

When people make mistakes they sometimes try to excuse their errors by saying, "Well, I didn't know *that* was wrong!"

Yeah . . . *riiiight!*

The truth is, if you are trying your best to be valiant, you'll *know* when you're on the wrong track. You'll *know* when you're doing wrong. If you are living worthy of the influence of the Holy Ghost, you'll feel little pangs of guilt. And those uncomfortable twitches will be the Holy Ghost telling you that you're going in the wrong direction.

Listen to them!

"People generally know when they are doing wrong," President Kimball once wrote. "Certainly all people who possess the Holy Ghost and who live worthy of its promptings will know when they enter the portals of sin" (*The Miracle of Forgiveness* [Salt Lake City: Bookcraft, 1969], 151).

If you ever do have doubts or questions about something you've done, talk with your parents. Visit with your bishop, your seminary teacher, or another respected adult. Ask your Father in Heaven, and "by the power of the Holy Ghost ye may know the truth of all things" (Moroni 10:5).

DESIRE TO CHANGE

The next step is wanting to change. It's wanting to be better, wanting to be the best you can be. It's wanting to live the commandments and to become more like your Father in Heaven.

Have you ever been sitting in general conference, sacrament meeting, or seminary and suddenly felt that you needed to improve some aspect of your life? When you felt that you *could* be better or that you *needed* to be better?

Act on those feelings! Let those little twitches spur you on to improve, to work harder, and to be better!

This is what Alma was explaining to his son Coriantum when he said, "Let your sins trouble you, with that trouble which shall bring you down unto repentance" (Alma 42:29).

You see, true repentance takes effort. And that means it doesn't happen unless you're willing to give it your best shot. You have to *want* to change.

GIVE IT UP

I once heard a comedian say, "It's easy to quit smoking. . . . I've done it hundreds of times!"

Unfortunately, that's exactly how some people approach repentance. For them, "giving up" a weakness means cutting down. Or quitting temporarily. But that's not the way it works. To truly repent of a weakness you must cut it out, completely and forever.

Imagine driving a car on a stormy day and bringing it home covered with mud. But instead of giving the car a good, paint-restoring wash and wax, suppose you simply sprayed off the tires. Or just polished the windows. Or merely rinsed off the hood.

Wouldn't that be silly?

Would your car ever become clean?

Of course not!

To make the car clean, you have to wash it completely and thoroughly. You have to rinse off the soap and dry it. You have to apply a good coat of wax to bring luster to the paint.

Repentance is like that. To repent of a sin, you must *give it up completely.* You have to shake it off and never look back.

Bishop Keith B. McMullin once said: "Make a mental list of those things you know you ought not to be doing. Stop doing today at least one such thing, and replace it with what you ought to do. Pray to Heavenly Father for forgiveness and for the strength to complete this journey. As you overcome one obstacle and move on to another, I promise that step by step the way will unfold before you until, as the wearied traveler, you are back where you belong" ("Welcome Home," *Ensign,* May 1999, 79).

RESIST TEMPTATION

I used to run a cross-country ski camp in the mountains of southern Utah. Part of our program involved skiing to the top of a scenic, 800-foot cliff we called the Overlook. To keep skiers a safe distance from the edge, we stuck broken ski poles in the snow as a barrier. Some daring skiers liked to ski right up to the edge of this safety zone, while others stayed a respectful distance back.

Many young people approach temptations much like that. Some believe that it's okay to approach the fringe of temptation as long as they don't go over the edge. They flirt with temptation, allowing themselves to approach the very edge of disaster, believing they can jump safely back when they need to.

And many times they can.

The thing you have to remember, though, is that it doesn't matter how many times you can get safely back. You have to cross the line only once to experience disaster.

"If you cross to the devil's side of the line one inch, you are in the tempter's power," President George Albert Smith warned, "and if he is successful, you will not be able to think or even reason properly, because you will have lost the Spirit of the Lord" (quoted by President James E. Faust, "The Enemy Within," *Ensign,* Nov. 2000, 45).

I know a young woman named Heather who had a birthday party in her home. She invited several young men and women, and she had wholesome games and tasty refreshments to keep everyone entertained. Heather was a talented artist, and after a while several of her girlfriends went to her bedroom to see the caricatures she had hanging on her wall. A few minutes later a few of the boys showed up to look, too.

"Sorry, guys," Heather said, shooing the boys back out the door. "*We* can be in here. And it's okay if you guys want to come in and look, too. But *you* can't be in here at the same time *we* are."

I was impressed when Heather told me that story. And when I asked her if that was a family rule she shook her head.

"No," she said. "It's just smart." And then she said something I've never forgotten: "If you don't go near the fire, you never get burned."

If you want to be worthy of the Spirit of the Lord, don't flirt with danger. Don't take chances. Avoid the very appearance of evil. Stay as far away from the edge of temptation as possible. And if you somehow find yourself in a precarious situation, you "can also emulate the spiritual reflexes of Joseph in Egypt: when he was tempted, 'he . . . fled' (Gen. 39:12), showing both courage and good legs!" (Elder Neal A. Maxwell, "The Tugs and Pulls of the World," *Ensign,* Nov. 2000, 36).

EXPERIENCE THE MIRACLE OF REPENTANCE

Having clean hands means being free of sin. But no one is perfect, and everyone makes mistakes. When those mistakes happen, correct them.

I remember a night on one of my cross-country ski trips. We were taking a trip deep into the mountains, and one young man was having a terrible time. Besides having a backpack that didn't fit him well, he had it stuffed to the point of bursting.

Finally, when it looked like he was never going to make it up a particularly steep hill, I said, "Look, Craig, why don't you take your pack off? I'll make sure it gets up to the lodge."

Craig looked at me with hopeful eyes. "Are you sure?"

"You bet! Don't worry about it."

With that, Craig dropped his pack and skied off.

I waited until he was around the bend, and then picked up his pack. I already had a pack of my own, so I carried mine on one shoulder and Craig's on the other. Talk about heavy! As I struggled up the mountain I felt like I was carrying a horse.

When I finally reached the lodge and dropped the packs, I felt as light as a feather. I went bouncing around the lodge like I had springs on my feet.

I felt fantastic!

Freeing yourself from the burden of sin is something like that, only better.

When I was working at a Boy Scout camp, we conducted what we called Honor Campfires. We talked about the meaning of honor and what it meant to live honorable lives. After the campfire each troop returned to its own campsite, where the Scouts had testimony meetings. These were always touching and spiritual, and many boys counted them as the highlight of their week.

One week a young man named Chase was in camp. He was so touched by the Spirit at his testimony meeting that afterwards he went looking for his Scout-master.

"I need to talk to the bishop," Chase said.

"Okay. I'm sure we can arrange an appointment on Sunday."

Chase shook his head. "No, you don't understand. I *need* to talk to him. *Right now.*"

The Scoutmaster looked at his watch. It was nearly ten o'clock.

At night.

Even so, the Scout leader sensed that Chase had been touched and that he did indeed need to speak to the bishop right away. They phoned home, and even though they were nearly an hour away, the bishop agreed to stay up to visit with Chase.

Chase returned to camp the next day. And even though I didn't know him well I could sense a difference. He was lighter and happier. He'd had a heavy burden lifted from him.

The prophet Isaiah wrote, "Come now, and let us reason together, saith the Lord: though your sins be as scarlet, they shall be as white as snow; though they be red as crimson, they shall be as wool" (Isaiah 1:18).

You, too, can cleanse yourself so that your hands and conscience are as clean and pure as newly fallen snow. So if you are burdened with past mistakes, follow the plan outlined by your Heavenly Father. Give them up, completely and forever. Confess your mistakes to your bishop, if they are serious. Pray for strength in resisting temptations and ask the Lord for forgiveness.

"The mission of the Church of Jesus Christ of Latter-day Saints is to call people everywhere to repentance," President Kimball said. "Those who heed the call . . . can be partakers of the miracle of forgiveness. . . . It is my hope and prayer that men and women everywhere will respond to this gentle invitation and thus let the Master work in their individual lives the great miracle of forgiveness" (*The Miracle of Forgiveness* [Salt Lake City: Bookcraft, 1969] 367–68).

Please don't wait another minute! Experience the great blessings and peace of mind that come from true repentance.

Get started now!

WARRIOR WORKOUT TIPS

- Take a good look at yourself. If you have habits that you know are bad, change them! Replace them with habits that bless and enrich your life, that make you happy, and that bring you closer to your Heavenly Father.
- If there are past mistakes you have not yet repented of, take care of them now! Pray for forgiveness. Make restitution, if you need to. Talk with your bishop, if necessary. Cleanse yourself so that *your* hands are clean and pure.
- Avoid temptations (see 1 Thessalonians 5:22). Stay away from people who might lead you astray. Avoid activities that might compromise your standards. Stay away from places that are not inviting to the Spirit of the Lord.
- Follow Bishop McMullin's advice and choose a commandment that you struggle with. Pray for help and strength in overcoming it. Make that particular weakness a strength in your life!

4

CANDY WRAPPERS ON THE FLOOR!

Becoming Pure in Heart

Brother Sanders, my tenth-grade seminary teacher, was at it again. He walked into the classroom chewing on a candy bar. Without a word, he tossed the wrapper on the floor and began his lesson.

Everyone loved Brother Sanders. He was an energetic teacher who helped all of us to build our testimonies and increase our love for the gospel. But today, no one was paying attention to him. Instead, everyone was focused on the wrapper in the middle of the floor. After all, Brother Sanders kept his classroom neat and orderly. A piece of garbage on the floor was as out of place as circus acts on Temple Square.

After several minutes a young woman named Amy stood to sharpen her pencil, and she picked up the wrapper on the way.

Without missing a beat, Brother Sanders produced another wrapper and casually tossed it to the floor.

The suspense was too much to bear. A student named Kim raised her hand.

"Yes, Kim?"

"Why are you doing that?"

Brother Sanders tried to appear innocent. "Doing what?"

Kim pointed. "Why do you keep throwing wrappers on the floor?"

The teacher shrugged. "Does that bother you?"

"Well, yeah!"

Brother Sanders shrugged again. "If it bothers you that much, pick it up!"

Kim sighed, stood from her desk, retrieved the wrapper, and threw it away.

Without a word, Brother Sanders threw another wrapper on the floor.

By now our teacher had everyone's undivided attention. Everyone knew he was trying to make a point, and we couldn't wait to find out what it was.

He finally spoke. "It's interesting," he said. "*One* little piece of garbage on the floor has you all in an uproar. But many of you tolerate *lots* of garbage in your minds. Garbage from filthy music. Garbage from vulgar movies. Garbage from impure thoughts."

He paused for a moment. "Why do you worry over a little thing like a candy wrapper on the floor, but allow *all kinds* of filth to pollute your minds? And your hearts?"

The class was silent. Brother Sanders had made his point so well that everyone was touched.

And he was right. It is so easy to let little bits of garbage pollute our hearts and minds. But it takes only a little to drive away the Spirit of the Lord. A single impure thought can become two, and then three. And together they keep us from focusing upon more important, more spiritual things. They weaken, dull, and even kill your spirit.

In the last chapter we discussed repentance and the importance of keeping your hands clean. So what more is there to do?

Let me give you an example.

Suppose that at the next session of general conference a new commandment were revealed: Thou shalt not eat chocolate.

Whoa!

No more chocolate?

Tough one! But being a valiant teenager, you immediately vow to never eat another bite. You throw away every candy bar in your school locker and even clean out the secret stash in your sock drawer. By doing this, by keeping yourself free of chocolate, you keep your *hands clean* (see Psalm 24:3–4).

But suppose that even though you quit *eating* chocolate, you never quite quit *thinking* about it. After all, you *love* chocolate! And every time you pass a candy machine you can't resist pausing to look over the wonderful, gooey selections. At night, you fall asleep dreaming of candy bars and hot fudge sundaes.

You see, abstaining from sin is only half the battle. That's having clean hands. Ridding yourself of the *thoughts* and *desires* for sin is the other half. And that's what it means to have a pure heart. And that's the hard part. It's so much easier to control your actions than your thoughts. It's so much easier to have clean hands than a pure heart. But you can rid yourself of ugly thoughts and desires so that your heart and mind are as clean and pure and "white as snow" (Isaiah 1:18).

How do you do that?

Let me share some steps.

DECIDE

The first step to becoming pure in heart is deciding that you sincerely *want* to be. It's not enough to simply believe that you *should* be. It's not enough to believe that you *ought* to be. You can only do it if you absolutely, honestly, 100 percent *want* to be.

Why?

Because it's hard! It's tough! And it's going to take your very best effort.

Elder Boyd K. Packer said: "Probably the greatest challenge to people of any age, particularly young people, and the most difficult thing you will face in mortal life is to learn to control your thoughts. As a man 'thinketh in his heart, so is he.' (Prov. 23:7.) One who can control his thoughts has conquered himself" ("Inspiring Music—Worthy Thoughts," *Ensign*, Jan. 1974, 25).

So if you truly want to become pure in heart, decide now. Make a commitment. Decide that being worthy of the Spirit of the Lord is important to you, and then resolve to do whatever it takes to achieve it.

Are you ready to do that?

Great!

Then the next step is to:

FIGHT

This is where the real effort comes in. This is where you'll find out just how much you want to keep your heart and mind pure. Anytime unworthy thoughts or desires creep into your mind, fight them! Resist them! Force them out of your mind!

This might seem like a tough thing, but you can do it. There are *no* temptations that are greater than you can bear (see 1 Corinthians 10:13, D&C 62:1).

Remember, too, that your mind can focus on only a single thought at a time. So if your mind is full of positive, uplifting thoughts, you have no room for the other kind. If you make a habit of thinking good thoughts, it will be easier to resist dark, ugly ones.

Elder Packer had this advice: "Choose from among the sacred music of the Church a favorite hymn, one with words that are uplifting and music that is reverent. . . . Go over it in your mind carefully. Memorize it. Even though you have had no musical training, you can think through a hymn.

"Now, use this hymn as the place for your thoughts

to go. . . . As the music begins and as the words form in your thoughts, the unworthy ones will slip shamefully away" ("Inspiring Music—Worthy Thoughts," *Ensign,* Jan. 1974, 25).

I love Elder Packer's advice because I know it works. I was hiking in the mountains one time. It was late at night, and I didn't have a flashlight. That shouldn't have been a problem except that I have an incredible imagination. And every time I heard a leaf crunch or a twig snap, I imagined all sorts of hairy, scary creatures sneaking up on me. After only a few minutes I became convinced that Bigfoot himself was homing in on me.

It was scary!

But I remembered Elder Packer's counsel. And I began singing hymns to myself. My favorites were the ones I first learned as a deacon in priesthood meeting, hymns like "How Firm a Foundation" and "We Thank Thee, O God, for a Prophet" (*Hymns,* 1985, nos. 85 and 19).

As I began singing to myself, two things happened. First, a calm, peaceful feeling settled over me. As I changed my focus from spooky thoughts to spiritual ones, I began to feel better.

Second, as I concentrated on the words of the

hymns, I was unable to think of spooky things. After all, your mind can focus on only one thing at a time. And with my mind filled with clean, wholesome thoughts, there was no room for spooky ones.

If you find impure, unworthy, or unclean thoughts sneaking into your mind, try singing a hymn. Or quote to yourself your favorite scripture. Try reciting the Articles of Faith. Think about your favorite heroes from the scriptures or Church history. Crowd your mind so full of good, uplifting thoughts that there isn't any room for anything else.

HAVING A CHANGE OF HEART

Singing hymns will help when ugly thoughts sneak into your mind. But if you are consumed with dark images, you might need to cleanse a little deeper. You might need to do some serious scouring in the depths of your soul, cleaning and polishing until all the dark spots are eliminated. This is what's known as having a change of heart (see Alma 5:13–14).

I like to read, and before my mission I sometimes read books that contained an occasional offensive word or scene. I'm embarrassed to admit it, but they were exactly the sort of thing Brother Sanders warned us about. I was so used to it that the coarse language didn't bother me. I scarcely even noticed offensive words when I read them.

After Brother Sanders's lesson I quit reading that sort of thing. But after I returned from my mission I one day picked up a book by a popular author.

Whammo!

Ugly words in the first paragraph jolted me like a punch in the face. I had become so sensitized to bad language that I couldn't even finish the first page. I threw the book away and haven't read that sort of thing since.

You see, my heart had *changed.* Words that had once not bothered or affected me now jolted me with an almost physical shock. And, in the same way, your heart can change, too. You can rid yourself of the darkest, basest of thoughts and temptations and fill your heart with goodness, richness, and light.

How long will it take? For Paul and Alma, the change happened overnight (which is pretty rare). For me it took two years on a mission. For most people it involves a long, deliberate effort. But as you work at it—as you work to become clean and pure—your Heavenly Father will notice and bless your efforts. The

Holy Ghost will give you strength, comfort, and guidance.

So if there are temptations you struggle with, temptations you'd like to wipe from your mind and your heart, ask your Heavenly Father for help. Fast, if you need to. Work at it. Ask for a priesthood blessing or visit with your bishop.

Elder Jeffrey R. Holland once said: "If you are struggling with self control . . . , I ask you to pray to your Father in Heaven for help. Pray to him as Enos did, who wrestled before God and struggled mightily in the Spirit. Wrestle like Jacob did with the angel, refusing to let go until a blessing had come. Talk to your mom and dad. Talk to your bishop. Get the best help you can from all the good people who surround you. Avoid at all costs others who would tempt you, weaken your will, or perpetuate the problem" ("Sanctify Yourselves," *Ensign,* Nov. 2000, 38).

Remember that the Savior wept and bled and died for you. He has given everything for your happiness and salvation. He certainly is not going to withhold help from you now. If you pray for help and guidance, you will receive it.

Elder Vaughn J. Featherstone said, "As the Comforter abides with us, we receive constant impressions and guidance, which, if followed, will lead us to become pure in heart" ("Pure of Heart," *New Era,* Aug. 1973, 5).

As you strive to be valiant, make the effort to purify your heart. Decide now that you'll do it. Work and fight and pray, and the Lord—your friend—will bless you. Don't wait another minute.

Start now!

Warrior Workout Tips

- Decide that you want—really *want*—to be pure in heart. Commit to doing whatever it takes to get there.
- Now choose a favorite hymn or scripture. Then, anytime ugly thoughts or desires try sneaking their way into your mind, think through the words. Don't let the ugly thoughts linger for a single *second!* Crowd your mind so full of good, uplifting thoughts that there is no room for anything else.
- Remember to pray for help. Be assured that your Father in Heaven will bless and help you. As you pray for help and guidance, the Holy Ghost will help you to find it.

5

WALKING OUT OF THE MOVIE!

Being Courageous

Chelsea Frost was in my first-period class. So when I returned to my room in the middle of lunch one day, I was surprised to find her sitting at my desk.

"Hey," I said. "How come you're not eating?"

"This isn't my lunch," she said. "I'm supposed to be in history."

"*Supposed* to be, huh? What happened?"

Chelsea looked embarrassed. "Well," she said, "Mr. Walker is showing a movie. And it's really bad. I didn't feel good watching it, so I left."

"Really?" I took a seat, anxious to hear the whole story.

"Oh, yeah," Chelsea said. "Mr. Walker warned us that it was graphic, but he said it had been approved by the district so it was okay to watch it." She shook her head. "But it's not. I only stayed for a minute, but I felt so uncomfortable that I knew I had to leave. I *knew* my mom wouldn't want me watching it."

"So you left?"

She nodded.

"What did Mr. Walker say? Was he mad?"

"Kinda. He said I wouldn't know the answers to the worksheet we have to do, and I wouldn't be able to participate in the discussion . . ."

"But you left anyway . . ."

She nodded.

Actually, I wasn't surprised. That's the sort of young woman Chelsea was. She wasn't afraid to stand up for what she believed in. She wasn't afraid to stick to her principles.

You see, being valiant often means having the courage to stand up for your convictions. It means being brave enough to do what you know is right, no matter what. It means being bold enough to share your testimony. Strong enough to do the things you know are right, even though others might laugh or ridicule.

One of my favorite stories involves Joseph F. Smith. In the fall of 1857, as he was returning from his mission to the Sandwich Islands, he was traveling through

California, where many people were not friendly to Mormons. One night as Joseph was gathering firewood, several drunken men rode into camp. They were waving pistols, swearing, and shouting threats at the Mormons they expected to find.

Joseph's companions had snuck out of camp and hidden in the trees. But Joseph thought to himself, *Why should I run? What do I have to worry about?*

And so—with his arms full of firewood—he marched straight into camp and up to the campfire.

One of the drunken men was storming around in a rage when he spotted Joseph. Brandishing his pistol in Joseph's face, he demanded, "Are you a Mormon?"

Joseph nodded and exclaimed, "Yes, siree! Dyed in the wool, true blue, through and through!"

I don't know what Joseph expected the man to do. But the man's response surprised him. The man grabbed Joseph by the hand and said: "Well, you are the pleasantest man I ever met! Shake, young fellow! I am glad to see a man that stands up for his convictions!" (*Gospel Doctrine* [Salt Lake City: Deseret Book, 1977], 518, 531–32).

I love that story. And I hope that, under similar

circumstances, I would have the courage to do the same thing.

I used to coach thirteen-year-old baseball players. One day, as I was getting to know everyone, I asked a boy named Kyle, "Are you LDS?"

Kyle grinned at me and said, "You're darn right! Are you?"

I loved Kyle's reply! He was proud of his beliefs, and he wasn't ashamed to let me know it. He wasn't afraid to stand up for himself. I have no doubt that if I had said no, he would have borne his testimony and offered me a Book of Mormon.

Now, what about you? When you're in a tough situation, how do *you* act? Do you let your light shine as an example to others? Are you courageous to stand by your convictions?

When the Prophet Joseph Smith told about his experience in the Sacred Grove, he was often tormented and ridiculed. But he never backed down from what he knew to be true. He said: "I was hated and persecuted for saying that I had seen a vision, yet it was true; and while they were persecuting me, reviling me, and speaking all manner of evil against me falsely for so saying, I was led to say in my heart: Why persecute me for telling the truth? I have actually seen a vision; and who am I that I can withstand God, or why does the world think to make me deny what I have actually seen? For I had seen a vision; I knew it, and I knew that God knew it, and I could not deny it, neither dared I do it; at least I knew that by so doing I would offend God, and come under condemnation" (Joseph Smith–History 1:25).

Was it hard for the prophet to tell what he saw?

Of course it was!

Did the reaction of others hurt him?

Of course it did!

Did that stop him from doing what he knew was right?

Of course not!

Though people mocked and tormented him for doing it, Joseph went about his Heavenly Father's business and "heeded them not" (1 Nephi 8:33).

When you are faced with an unpleasant situation, be strong! Stand up for what you know is right. Follow the words of the song and "do what is right; let the consequence follow" (*Hymns,* 1985, no. 237).

I have a young friend named Brandon who spent one summer working with a construction crew. He was the newest member of the crew—and the youngest—

and he was anxious to be accepted by the older, more experienced men.

But one afternoon, when the conversation became cheap and ugly, Brandon knew that he couldn't stand idly by. Gathering up all the courage he had, he said, "Guys, I really don't like listening to this. Would you mind talking about something else?"

Most of the men seemed surprised to hear Brandon speak up. And one man looked at him with a belittling grin and said something about not offending the "little mama's boy."

Brandon said that he could have died on the spot. But he stood his ground. He looked the man straight in the eye and said: "That's right. But you know what? I've been telling my mom what great guys you are to work with. I tell her how much I'm learning from you. I tell her what great examples you are." And then he lowered his voice and said, "I just don't want her to be disappointed."

Brandon said doing that was the scariest thing he'd ever done. And he fully expected to be teased about it, or maybe even switched to another crew.

"But it didn't happen," he said. "They kept me on

the crew for the rest of the summer. And they never, *ever,* talked that way around me again."

Elder Dean L. Larsen once said, "The nature of the challenges we face in this life is not nearly so important as what we choose to do about them. When we have the courage and faith to live up to the best we know, we fulfill the purpose for which we came to this earth, and we provide an incentive for others to do the same" ("Faith, Courage, and Making Choices," *Ensign,* Nov. 1978, 34).

I know a young man named Tim who one day overheard several boys talking in the locker room about a young woman named Jenny. The conversation was ugly and offensive. And Tim decided that he wasn't going to let it continue.

"Knock it off!" he demanded. "Jenny's a friend of mine, and nothing you've said about her is true. I'm *not* gonna stand here and let you talk about her like that!"

"Oh, yeah?" one of the boys challenged. "What are you gonna do about it?"

Tim stood his ground. "I'll tell you what," he said. "The first thing I'm gonna do is tell the coach. You know he doesn't tolerate that kind of talk. And then I'm gonna tell Jenny, too. I think she ought to know what kind of friends you guys are."

Now *that* took a lot of courage! And it made a difference. The boys changed their conversation. And later, one of them even went looking for Tim.

"Hey," he said. "I'm sorry. We were way out of line in there. I like Jenny, too. And I shouldn't have let the guys go on like that."

You might not think about it, but you face situations every day that require courage. And how you react is a good indication of where you stand in your efforts to be valiant.

What do you do, for instance, when you're with friends and the conversation becomes offensive? Do you have the courage to ask everyone to change the subject? Or to walk away?

Or what do you do when you're watching movies with friends and someone brings a video that you know your parents wouldn't approve of? Are you brave enough to tell them that you don't want to watch? Are you bold enough to suggest watching—or doing—something else?

It's tough!

But be assured that when you act with courage,

when you stand up for your convictions, your Heavenly Father will notice.

When I was a missionary in Japan, many elders began using very "generic" approaches when they knocked on doors. Rather than identify themselves as missionaries, they'd say things like, "We have a family-oriented message to share." Or, "We're visiting the neighborhood showing a filmstrip about families."

Many elders even quit wearing their official name tags.

I have to admit that for a time, I was one of these.

Then I was assigned a brand-new elder as my companion. He was young and excited and eager to learn. He quickly learned all the approaches I taught him. Then one day he said, "Elder Barker, would you do me a favor?"

"Sure," I said. "What is it?"

"I'd like you to teach me a new approach."

"Like what?"

"I don't know," he said. "But I want to tell people that I'm a missionary. And that I want to teach them about Jesus Christ."

"Hmmmm," I said. "I'll have to think of one. I mean, it's been a long time since I've done that."

But I agreed. I made up a new approach and we used it all day. At every door we said: "Good morning! We represent The Church of Jesus Christ of Latter-day Saints, and we'd like to share with you an important message about Jesus Christ."

That day we talked with more people than ever. The next day we talked with even more. And before long elders from all over the mission were calling to ask what our secret was.

I learned a great lesson from my companion. I learned the importance of standing up for who I was and not being afraid to share my convictions or testimony.

"Today it requires great courage to be a loyal Latter-day Saint," Elder Larsen said. "For many it is not easy, and it will likely not become easier. The tests of our day are severe. . . .

"You . . . have a tremendous trust placed in you by the Lord, and he expects you to measure up—to stand up and be counted. All of you came here to be winners. The Lord's work will prevail, and you will have much to do with the success of his kingdom" ("Faith, Courage, and Making Choices," *Ensign,* Nov. 1978, 34).

Remember the words of the song, "Do what is

right; let the consequence follow!" As you do, as you stand up for your convictions and choose the right, the Lord will watch over you and protect you. He'll bless you for your courage. And you will truly know the joy of being a valiant servant of your Father in Heaven.

WARRIOR WORKOUT TIPS

- When tough situations come up in your life, be brave. Do the right thing, no matter what happens!
- Be proud of who you are and what you believe. Never be ashamed to say that the gospel of Jesus Christ is important to you.
- Remember that many times others will feel just as you do. If you have the courage to walk away from a compromising situation, if you are brave enough to stand up for what you believe, others may find the courage to follow your example.

6

BURIED IN THE SNOW!

Being an Example

"See this guy? He's the reason I'm going to serve a mission."

Jeff Russell, a ninth grader in my geometry class, showed me a picture. It was of a young man in a suit; the teenager looked clean-cut and sharp looking, but other than that he seemed fairly ordinary.

"Who is he?" I asked.

"One of my football coaches," Jeff said. "He just got his mission call. I was planning on serving a mission anyway, but now Nick's got me *really* pumped up about it."

"Really?" I asked. "How'd he do that?"

"Just by being such a good example," Jeff said. "And he's always telling us how excited he is to go."

I was impressed that Nick had such an influence on

Jeff. But it wasn't just Jeff. I talked with other players who had been influenced as much as Jeff. I finally asked one of them, "What makes this guy so special?"

"He's a great coach," a boy named Danny told me. "And he has an incredible testimony. It's really powerful."

"How do you know that?"

"Because he bore it to us."

"He bore his testimony?" I asked. "At *football?*"

"Oh, yeah," Danny said. "After our last game. He told us that he knew the gospel was true and he challenged all of us to serve missions."

I had to ask. "So are you planning on a mission?"

Danny nodded emphatically. "You bet I am!"

That experience had a profound impact on me. I was impressed that the young coach had such an influence on his players. And even though he didn't know it, his influence spread far beyond his football team. As I thought about my conversations with Jeff, Danny, and all of the other boys, I realized that I envied Nick. I was a coach myself. And I wished that I inspired my players as much as Nick inspired his. I decided right then and there that I would do everything I could to motivate and inspire *my* players to be valiant young men and to begin preparing to serve missions.

Nick's example was so powerful that he influenced me—someone he'd never met—*and* all of the boys I coached.

Now, you set an example, too. Whether you realize it or not, people watch you. They see the way you talk and the way you act, and many of them follow your lead. And that's good, because your Heavenly Father needs young men and women who set good examples for their peers. He needs young people who can influence their friends and associates to be better people.

"Just as it is difficult for a weary sailor to find his way across uncharted seas without the aid of a compass, it is almost impossible for . . . youth to find their way through the seas of life without the guiding light of a good example," said Elder Russell M. Ballard. " . . . It is our solemn duty to set a powerful, personal example of righteous strength, courage, sacrifice, unselfish service, and self-control. These are the traits that will help . . . youth hold on to the iron rod of the gospel and remain on the straight and narrow path" ("Like a Flame Unquenchable," *Ensign,* May 1999, 85).

I know a young woman named Brittan who was at girls' camp. One evening several of her friends were sitting around and discussing their camping partners.

"I can't believe Melissa came again this year," one young woman said. "She doesn't like any of the activities and she never does anything but complain."

"I *know!*" another camper exclaimed. "And Kelli's the same way! She takes the fun out of everything!"

As the conversation continued, Brittan squirmed uncomfortably. She didn't like hearing her friends being so critical of others. *They* were starting to take the fun out of everything. So when the group was about to vote on the most annoying girl at camp that year, she said: "Hey! You know what? We ought to vote on the most *inspirational* girl! Then maybe we could secretly give her an award or something."

"Yes!" someone else chimed in. "And maybe we could vote on the most spiritual."

"And the most fun!"

"And the best dressed!"

At this last suggestion, everyone laughed. But just like that, everyone's mood had changed. The girls cast their votes and spent the rest of the week sneaking secret notes and prizes to their friends, making camp even more fun for everyone.

With a single, simple suggestion Brittan changed everyone's attitude. She changed a negative situation into an experience that was fun, positive, and uplifting for everyone.

Now, what about you? Are you setting an example that is good, clean, and uplifting? Can your friends see by your actions that the gospel is an important part of your life? Can they tell that you live the Word of Wisdom? Think about the language you use, the stories you tell, and the movies you watch. Think about the way you dress. Do you look like a servant of your Heavenly Father? Is there any doubt about where you stand in the battle for righteousness?

I have a young friend named Christy who went to a community dance. Many of her friends were there, as were teenagers from all over town. But it was only a few minutes before Christy realized it wasn't an event her parents would approve of.

"The music was loud and wild," she told me. "They were playing the kind of songs that they're always warning us about in seminary, and they weren't enforcing any kind of dress standards. People were wearing things that they don't even allow in school. It was a bad atmosphere, and I felt really uncomfortable being there."

Christy told her friends how she was feeling, telling

them: "I really don't feel good being here. I don't think we should stay."

At first, only two of Christy's friends seemed to agree with her. But when they saw that Christy really was going to leave, several others decided to go, too.

"We didn't have a ride so we had to walk home," Christy said. "But we had the best time! We went back to my house and guess what? A bunch of the guys came over, too. They didn't like what was happening any more than we did. We ended up eating ice cream and playing games and having a great time."

Christy's eyes gleamed as she told me the story.

"But the best part," she said, "was that later a bunch of kids told me thanks for leaving. They said they wanted to leave, too, but just didn't want to be the first one to say something."

You see, there may be times when *your* friends need someone to lead the way, too. So be that person! Be the one brave enough to do what's right. Be the one who takes the first step so that others can follow. You never know when your example might change a life.

When I was on my mission I once had a companion who was the most highly charged, optimistic, gung-ho, ready-to-get-out-and-baptize missionary I ever knew. *Nothing* ever got him down.

I remember waking up one soggy, drizzly morning and looking out the window. *Oh, great,* I thought. *Rain. This is going to be a wonderful day!*

Missionary work was always hard in the rain because we had to ride our bikes everywhere we went. And even though we had rain suits and umbrellas, we always ended up getting soaked to the skin.

Besides that, not many people enjoyed inviting rain-soaked strangers into their homes, so meeting new people was difficult.

I was just gearing myself up for a long, miserable day when Elder Kelly came bouncing out of the bathroom.

"Elder Barker!" he boomed. "Isn't it great? It's *raining!* Everyone's going to be home today! We're going to meet *hundreds* of people!"

I couldn't help grinning at my companion's attitude. But he cheered me up. He made me feel better. And when he started singing the missionary song from *Saturday's Warrior,* I couldn't help breaking down and singing with him. Instead of being gloomy and cheerless, we charged into the rain determined to have the best day ever. And we did!

You can have the same effect on the people *you* know.

So when your Young Women's advisor announces a service project, smile! Show by your example that you're excited to serve your Father in Heaven. Use your good attitude to motivate, inspire, and energize everyone around you!

If the talk in the locker room becomes crude or foul, change the subject. Start talking about last night's ball game or the upcoming school dance. Steer the conversation toward positive, uplifting topics that generate excitement and enthusiasm.

No matter where you are or what you're doing, you can be an example to those around you. You can influence others to be good, to be better, and to be valiant, simply by showing them the way. You can be like the Savior, who said, "I am the light; I have set an example for you" (3 Nephi 18:16).

In an earlier chapter I mentioned once being caught in an avalanche. One sixteen-year-old boy named Nathan was buried up to his neck in the snow. As ski guides frantically began searching for missing skiers, several of Nathan's friends skied up and began digging him from the snow. It was dark and cold and—worst of all—no one knew if more snow was going to slide. The boys all knew they were risking their very lives being out in the open, but they knew they had to help their friend. Everyone was terrified, and one boy even began to cry.

But then an interesting thing happened. Nathan began to sing softly: "I am a child of God . . ."

The effect was electric. The feelings of fear and terror were suddenly replaced by a sense of peace and calm.

" . . . has given me an earthly home, with parents kind and dear . . ."

Even the boy who had been crying was digging now. It took several minutes, but Nathan was finally able to wiggle out of the snow. His example of calm and courage inspired his rescuers and helped to save his own life.

There are many wonderful examples we can follow in this world. Parents, for instance. And ward and seminary leaders. But your Heavenly Father needs people *your* age to be examples, too. He needs young people like you to help show the way to others who might need a guiding hand.

Be one of them!

Be an example!

WARRIOR WORKOUT TIPS

- Think about the way you act around other people. Think about the things you say. Are your words and actions a good example for others? If they're not, improve them!
- Always look for the best in people and situations. Never gossip or criticize.
- Always be positive and optimistic. Be happy! When you're faced with problems or challenges, look for solutions rather than someone to blame. Be someone your friends can turn to when they need a shot of enthusiasm or energy.
- Never think that you're too young to influence others. Remember the words of the Apostle Paul to his young friend Timothy: "Let no man despise thy youth; but be thou an example of the believers, in word, in conversation, in charity, in spirit, in faith, in purity" (1 Timothy 4:12).

7

FALLING OFF THE CLIFF

Developing Integrity

Shannon Evans waited until after class and then came up to talk.

"Hi," she said. "Can I talk to you about my test score?"

"Sure," I said, taking her test and looking it over. "Oh, yeah . . . see here? This is a tangent problem, but you set it up as cosine. And then right here? You added these two numbers when you should have multiplied."

"Oh, I already figured that out," Shannon said. "They were dumb mistakes. But I missed two problems, right?"

"Uh-huh."

"And I still got 96 percent?"

"Ah," I said, finally figuring it out. "You think your score is too *high,* don't you?"

She nodded.

"Okay, then . . . see here and here? You went a couple of steps further than you needed to. I really didn't expect anyone to understand that part yet, but I added a few extra points for everyone who did."

She brightened. "Really?"

"Yeah." I looked at her a little more closely. "You really were worried that your score was too high, weren't you?"

She nodded. "I just wanted the score I earned."

I was impressed. Whenever students believe that I haven't given them all the points they deserve on a test or quiz, they are usually quick to tell me about it. But it isn't often that someone tells me that I've given them too *many* points.

On the other hand, that's just the sort of young woman Shannon was (and, I'm certain, still is). She would rather miss being on the honor roll than receive grades that she didn't deserve.

That's integrity.

I used to run a Cub Scout camp. One afternoon a nine-year-old boy came up and told me that he'd lost ten dollars.

"No one's turned it in," I told him. "But check back

before you leave. There's a good chance someone will find it by then."

"Okay," he said. Then he handed me a five-dollar bill. "Here's this, though. I found it on the trail."

I was confused. "Wait," I said. "You lost ten dollars. But you found five?"

He nodded. "Uh-huh."

"And this isn't the money you lost?"

"I lost dollar bills," he said. "So that's not mine."

That was one of the most inspiring moments I've ever had at Scout camp. But the exciting thing was that it happened all the time. Boys were constantly bringing me knives, slides, rings, and money that they'd found on the trails. One time a boy ran up to me, handed me a wad of money, and then ran off again. When I unfolded it I discovered a total of twenty-two dollars. When I ran into the boy later, I asked him, "Do you know how much money you gave me?"

He shook his head. "I didn't count it," he said. "It wasn't mine, so I just gave it to you."

Those boys, and many others just like them, made an impression on me. There have been times since when I've been in similar situations, and I've always tried to follow their example.

When I was a student at BYU, I remember hearing that the campus lost-and-found was filled with pencils. *Pencils!*

Can you imagine that? Students so honest that when they picked up a pencil they actually went to the trouble to turn it in to lost-and-found?

On the other hand, that's exactly what we're talking about here.

"In all this world there is no substitute for personal integrity," said President Gordon B. Hinckley. "It includes honor. It includes performance. It includes keeping one's word. It includes doing what is right regardless of the circumstances" (*Teachings of Gordon B. Hinckley,* 1997, 270).

I recently read about a high school quarterback in Illinois by the name of Nate Haasis. During the last game of the season he was on the verge of breaking the conference career-passing record. In the last minute of the game—without telling Nate—the coaches of the two teams struck a deal. Nate's team would let the other team score if the other team would let Nate complete his last pass to break the record.

The plan went off without a hitch . . . except for one thing: Nate found out about it. Nate immediately wrote a letter to league officials asking that the pass not be included among the conference records.

"There'd always be a 'but' on his record," one of Nate's friends said. "And he didn't want that."

With that one act, Nate turned down an opportunity that he'd never, *ever*, have again. But his personal integrity was worth more to him than a record he didn't really earn.

You can be that way, too. You can be known for being completely, totally honest. You start by being honest with yourself, honest with others, and honest with your Heavenly Father.

What does that mean?

Let's break it down a little.

BEING HONEST WITH YOURSELF

Have you ever been in a questionable situation and found yourself making excuses about why it was okay to be there? Maybe you were watching a movie that you knew the prophet wouldn't approve of. *But,* you told yourself, it was okay because you planned to close your eyes during the bad parts.

Or maybe one of your friends began telling crude

stories. But, you told yourself, you weren't going to tell any yourself.

Or maybe you found yourself thinking that it was okay to miss paying your tithing one month because you *really* needed the money. Or that it was okay to miss sacrament meeting because it was "only" testimony meeting.

That's rationalizing. You start making excuses to yourself because, deep inside, you know that what you're doing is wrong. And so you make up things to justify your actions.

A student at school once brought me a calculator he'd found in the hall.

"Can I keep this?" he asked.

"I don't know," I said. "Have you tried to figure out who it belongs to?"

"Well, there's no name on it . . ."

I laughed. Most of the calculators I see don't have names on them. "We could ask around," I suggested.

"We're never gonna find out who owns it," he insisted.

"How do you know until you try?"

He shrugged. "Oh, all right . . ."

We never did find out who the calculator belonged

to. But Jon had begun making excuses so he wouldn't even have to try.

Be honest with yourself!

If you find yourself making excuses for something, chances are it's because it's something you shouldn't be doing. Those little pangs of guilt are the Holy Ghost telling you something. You'll feel better if you quit and do something else. Leave the movie. Turn off the TV. Change the conversation. Pay your tithing.

If you want to be honest with others and with your Heavenly Father, begin by being honest with yourself.

BEING HONEST WITH OTHERS

I know a young woman named Jordyn who was shopping. Being good with numbers, she had an idea how much she'd have to pay before she got to the checkout line. But to her surprise, the clerk asked for several dollars less.

"Is any of this on sale?" Jordyn asked.

The clerk shook her head. "No, not that I'm aware of."

"I was expecting to pay more than this."

Together, Jordyn and the clerk double checked the

figures, discovering that the total was correct. Jordyn had simply overestimated.

Still, I was proud of her for her honesty. She didn't believe she was being asked to pay the correct amount, and she didn't want to cheat anyone.

A young man named Kyle once told me about a time he'd gone snowboarding. He was twelve years old but looked much younger. One of his friends picked up the lift passes, and Kyle was surprised to see that his had the word "freebie" written on it.

"What's this?" he asked.

"Kids under eleven get in free," his friend said. "I told 'em you were ten."

"But we can't do that!"

"Sure we can. You look ten. And it saves us thirty-five dollars."

It was a lot of money. Even so, Kyle didn't feel good about cheating someone. Even when his friend tried to convince him that he really wasn't hurting anyone, Kyle threw away the free pass and bought himself a regular ticket.

Being honest with others often requires humbling yourself. And sometimes it even means suffering some embarrassment.

I used to help coach a seventh-grade football team. Our practices sometimes went on after dark, even when it was too dark to see the football.

"It's kind of pointless," a player named Brett told me one night as I gave him a ride home. "We can't even see!"

"And it's dangerous," I added. "If we have to practice three hours a night, we really ought to start earlier instead of staying so late."

A couple of nights later the head coach took me aside.

"Brett told me that you think our practices are dangerous," he said.

Oh, boy! I thought. *Brett wasn't supposed to repeat that!*

I was trapped. I hadn't meant to criticize the coach. And my first reaction was to act innocent, like I didn't know what he was talking about. But that wouldn't have been fair to Brett.

"Well, yeah," I said, finally. And then I apologized. "Look, Steve, I shouldn't have said that. I wasn't trying to criticize you behind your back."

It was pretty embarrassing.

When you find yourself in a situation like that, be

honest. Be up front about what you might have said or done.

Better yet, avoid getting into corners like that in the first place.

BEING HONEST WITH YOUR HEAVENLY FATHER

I once heard a story about a man who slipped and fell off a cliff. He prayed frantically as he tumbled through the sky, promising to repent and change his life if the Lord would just save him. Suddenly the branch of a tree snagged his coat and stopped his fall, saving his life.

The man took a moment to calm down, and then he finished his prayer.

"Um, never mind," he said. "I've got everything under control."

You can't fool your Heavenly Father. But some people still try. They might pray for forgiveness, for instance, when they're not really sorry about what they've done. They might not tell the whole story when talking with the bishop. In prayer, they might pledge to do their best at something, knowing that they really won't.

In times of need, many people approach the Lord and try bargaining. Like the man falling off the cliff, they say, "Please help me now, and I *promise* I'll start doing better!"

It's much better to live well now, so that you're always worthy of blessings when you need them. Then you can honestly, sincerely say: "I've kept myself clean. I've done what I should. Please help me now."

When virtue garnishes your thoughts unceasingly, your confidence will be strong in the presence of God (see D&C 121:45). When you are doing what is right, you won't feel timid or hesitant about asking the Lord for help. You will know that the Lord will hear and answer your prayers.

When you talk with your Heavenly Father, be honest. If you pray for help with some problem and don't do your part, fess up. Admit your mistakes and shortcomings, and then pray for help in overcoming them.

As you strive to be a modern stripling warrior, as you work to be honest with yourself, with others, and with your Heavenly Father, your personal integrity will grow and increase. But there's more you can do. You can keep your promises, for instance. You can be dependable, doing your chores and homework without being asked. You can be truthful, always remembering that even little "white" lies are dishonest. You can do your best work in school, never cheating or copying someone else's work.

As you do these things you will find yourself blessed in many ways.

"The rewards of integrity are immeasurable," said Elder Joseph B. Wirthlin. "One is the indescribable inner peace and serenity that come from knowing we are doing what is right; another is an absence of the guilt and anxiety that accompany sin. . . . [But] the consummate reward of integrity is the constant companionship of the Holy Ghost (see D&C 121:46). The Holy Ghost does not attend us when we do evil. But when we do what is right, he can dwell with us and guide us in all we do" ("Personal Integrity," *Ensign,* May 1990, 30).

Decide now to make integrity a personal goal. Be honest with yourself. Be honest with others. Be honest with your Heavenly Father. Discover how honesty and integrity can bless and enrich your life. Discover how they will drive you toward your goal of being a valiant teenager and becoming a latter-day stripling warrior.

WARRIOR WORKOUT TIPS

- Vow to be honest—completely, totally honest—in everything you do.
- Be dependable. Prove by your actions that people can count on you. Do your chores and homework without being asked. Keep your promises when you make them. Follow through on commitments you make. Always finish what you start.
- Do your own work at school. Never cheat or copy another person's work.
- If you have a job, always do your best work. Be a worker that your boss can always count on, not someone he has to keep an eye on.
- Apologize when you make mistakes. Admit it when you've been wrong. Take responsibility for your actions; never try to put the blame on someone else.
- Follow the example of the stripling warriors who "were men who were true at all times in whatsoever thing they were entrusted" (Alma 53:20). Conduct yourself so that the same thing can *always* be said of you!

8

THE MAN WITH THE HUNDRED-THOUSAND-DOLLAR NOSE

Living the Word of Wisdom

Fourteen-year-old Nathan Conrad peeled off his ski coat and stood looking down at himself like he was dressed in something old and moldy.

"Look at me!" he said. "I'm soaked all the way to the skin!"

"Me, too," Colby Dixon chimed in. "The last time I was this wet I was in a swimming pool!"

I dropped my gloves and heard a soggy *splat* as they hit the floor. We had just spent the morning snowboarding. It was snowing hard—snowing the really wet, slushy kind of snow—and even our heavy-duty ski coats weren't enough to keep us dry. After just a couple of runs we were sopping wet and had to retreat to the lodge to dry off and warm up. Within minutes, wisps of steam were curling off our clothes, and our fingers tingled as they warmed up.

I sniffed and looked at Colby, whose hands were wrapped around a cup of something warm and chocolate looking. I sniffed again.

"What are you drinking, Colby?"

Colby blew gently into his cup, and then took a long sip. "Hot chocolate," he said. "French vanilla."

"French vanilla? Where'd you get it?"

He pointed. "From the machine. Over there."

I had to squint to see the machine on the other side of the lodge. But then I laughed as I figured it out.

"Colby, . . . that's *coffee!*"

"Coffee?"

"Well, cappuccino—same thing."

Colby grimaced in horror. "Coffee? Oh, *yuck!*"

"Oh, just take it back," Nathan told him with a laugh. "Just tell 'em you goofed, and they'll let you get something else."

Holding the cup like it was full of night crawlers, Colby trudged off to the cash register.

Nathan grinned at me. "I can't wait to tell Brother Marshall about this one."

"Who's that?" I asked. "Your seminary teacher?"

Nathan nodded, and then deepened his voice in his best imitation of his teacher. "Class, I wanted to talk about Moroni today, but for Colby's sake we're going to have a Word of Wisdom refresher lesson."

I laughed. During the short morning Colby had already had several mishaps, and the cappuccino adventure was just keeping in character.

"I've never broken the Word of Wisdom," Nathan said.

"Really?" I asked. "Never?"

"Never." He shrugged. "I've seen kids smoke and stuff, but"—he pulled a face—"that's stupid. I don't know why anyone would want to do that."

I nodded in admiration. I've known other young men and women who have never broken the Word of Wisdom, and I've always admired them. One of the reasons we came to this earth was to get a body. It's one of the greatest gifts we have. Our Heavenly Father has taught us how to take care of it, and I have tremendous respect and admiration for young people who obey him.

President Hinckley once said: "We are made in [God's] image. These remarkable and wonderful bodies are His handiwork. Does anyone think that he can deliberately injure and impair his body without affronting its Creator? We are told again and again that the body is the tabernacle of the spirit. We are told that it is a temple, holy to the Lord" ("The Scourge of Illicit Drugs," *Ensign,* Nov. 1989, 48).

At the beginning of this chapter I wrote about snowboarding. I don't know if you've ever tried snowboarding, but I love it! I love slicing my board through fresh powder, carving through steep moguls, and zipping through tight, tricky tree trails. It makes me feel good, and a day in the snow fires me up for a long week at work.

The only problem is that bad knees run in my family. And it scares me to think that my knees might someday give out and end my snowboarding career. It scares me enough that I do special exercises all year long to strengthen my knees, just to keep them in shape for snowboarding.

Does that sound silly?

Rock star Bruce Springsteen knows what I'm talking about. He values his voice so much that he has it insured for more than *five million dollars!*

Lord of the Dance star Michael Flatley knows, too. He has his legs insured for *forty* million.

And Jimmy Durante, an old-time entertainer who had an unusual nose, had his nose insured for more than a hundred thousand dollars.

His *nose!*

Your body is so much more than your knees, voice, legs, or nose. It is a miracle that the world's best scientists cannot duplicate. And your Heavenly Father has given you instructions for taking care of it.

Follow them!

Get Enough Sleep

When people talk about the Lord's instructions for our bodies, they most often refer to things the Word of Wisdom says we shouldn't do. But just as important are the things we *should* do. Like getting enough sleep.

Elder Harold G. Hillam once said: "It's true, there's nothing in Section 89 about how much rest we have each night, but go back a couple of pages to Doctrine and Covenants 88:124: 'Cease to sleep longer than is needful; retire to thy bed early, that ye may not be weary; arise early, that your bodies and your minds may be invigorated'" ("Not For the Body," *Ensign,* Oct. 2001, 18).

Near the city of Orem, where I live, is a mountain called Timpanogos. At the top is a snowfield that never completely melts. At the bottom of that glacier is an emerald-blue lake fed by the melting snow.

Think that water's cold?

If you can imagine liquid ice, you'll have a pretty good idea of what the water in Emerald Lake feels like.

When I was an assistant Scoutmaster, my troop once climbed to the top of Timp, and then slid down the glacier. As we were eating our lunches near the lake, our troop clown said to me, "I bet you don't dare jump in the water . . ."

Yeah, I know what you're thinking. But it was a furnace-hot day, and I was hot and sticky from hiking. I thought a quick splash would be just the thing to spark me up and get me going again.

And so, with everyone in the troop egging me on, I walked to the edge of the lake and jumped in.

The next instant I came blasting out of the water like a missile shot from a submarine. I was so cold it took me several minutes before I could breathe normally, but you know what? I was *invigorated!* I'm not sure if I ever knew exactly what that word meant before, but I knew it then! Once I got my heart restarted I felt like a million bucks. I felt awake and alive and ready to climb another mountain. I felt like I could have outwrestled a grizzly bear and beaten Bigfoot in the 100-yard dash.

If you want to be at your best—if you want to do your best at work or at school—be sure you're getting enough sleep. Go to bed early. Get up early. Get the rest you need for your mind and body to be invigorated.

GET ENOUGH EXERCISE

Doctors and health experts around the world can tell you about the benefits of regular exercise. And President Ezra Taft Benson agreed with them: "Rest and physical exercise are essential, and a walk in the fresh air can refresh the spirit. Wholesome recreation is part of our religion and is a necessary change of pace; even its anticipation can lift the spirit" ("Do Not Despair," *Ensign,* Oct. 1986, 2).

Remember *that* the next time you're feeling down!

Several years ago I adopted a dog I named Trapper. Because I have to leave her alone for most of the day, I began taking her for long walks in the morning before work. It wasn't long before our walks became one of the best parts of my day. Besides being good exercise, it *did* refresh me. It put me in a good mood and helped to set the tone for the rest of the day. I noticed that I never felt quite as good on those days that we didn't start out with a brisk walk.

BE VALIANT IN ACTIVITY

Remember the stripling warriors? They were valiant teenagers. The Book of Alma records, "They were all young men, and they were exceedingly valiant for courage, and also for strength and *activity*" (Alma 53:20; emphasis added).

I think there's a great, often overlooked message in that verse. Be valiant in *activity*. What does that mean?

I think it means turning off the TV and getting out of the house. I think it means spending more time running and jumping than sitting in front of television or computer screens. I think it means doing things that get your heart beating and your blood pumping and make you feel good. Things like a game of basketball. A run through the park. A good hobby.

Be active! Find good hobbies that give you a lift and recharge your spirit. Play games that exercise your mind and body. Keep yourself busy with fun, wholesome activities.

KEEP THE SABBATH DAY HOLY

The Sabbath day? In a chapter on the Word of Wisdom?

Absolutely!

After creating the heaven and the earth, the Lord rested. And he has commanded us to do the same. Of course, there are many reasons for that, including great benefits for our spiritual and physical health.

Elder James E. Faust said that one reason the Lord has asked us to honor the Sabbath is because of our physical need for rest and renewal.

"Obviously God, who created us, would know more than we do of the limits of our physical and nervous energy and strength," he said. Elder Faust added that keeping the Sabbath holy would also satisfy our "need for regeneration and the strengthening of our spiritual being" ("The Lord's Day," *Ensign,* Nov. 1991, 33).

Of course, these are not the only—or even the most important—reasons for keeping the Sabbath day holy. But there is no question that doing so will benefit your physical and spiritual health. It will help you to be a more valiant teenager.

DON'TS

I'm sure that if you had a paper and pencil handy you could quickly make a list of things prohibited by the Word of Wisdom. You'd quickly list things like coffee, tea, tobacco, alcohol, and illegal drugs. You already know that those things are bad for you. But let me share this thought of Elder Theodore M. Burton: "As the Creator of man, [the Lord] *knows* which things are good for our bodies and which things are injurious to us. Jesus Christ as the God of this world has told us that alcoholic beverages, tobacco, tea, and coffee are all destructive to our health. The continued use of these substances will cause us misery and sorrow. They are not only injurious to our health, but actually destructive of our bodies and minds. . . . I repeat that the use of tobacco, tea, coffee, and alcoholic beverages of any kind is not only displeasing to the Lord, but also destructive of your body and mind" ("The Word of Wisdom," *Ensign,* May 1976, 28).

President Hinckley added: "You cannot afford to drink beer and other liquors which can rob you of self-control. You cannot afford to smoke cigarettes or use other forms of tobacco and live up to the values which the Lord has set for your guidance. The partaking or distribution of illegal drugs is to be shunned as you would shun a terrible disease" ("A Chosen Generation," *New Era,* Jan. 1999, 4).

Another time, he said: "To you who may be partaking, I repeat, stop immediately. To you who at any time in the future may be tempted, I urge you to stand your ground. . . . Do not throw away your future. Do not jeopardize the well-being of your posterity" ("The Scourge of Illicit Drugs," *Ensign,* Nov. 1989, 48).

There's no question that some things are bad for us and definitely violate the spirit of the Word of Wisdom. But there is a gray area, too, that sometimes causes problems. I once overheard a couple of young men, for instance, arguing over whether cola drinks violated the Word of Wisdom.

"After all," one boy said with a shrug of his shoulders, "they're not mentioned in the Doctrine and Covenants."

His friend snorted and said: "So what? Illegal drugs are not mentioned, either."

The truth is, the scriptures do not contain a complete list of prohibited items. The Lord revealed the Doctrine and Covenants 89 in answer to a specific question Joseph Smith asked about tobacco. It was never intended as the final word of dos and don'ts. But you have been taught values based upon the scriptures. Modern prophets have added additional guidance and counsel. You need to base your decisions upon them.

Elder Boyd K. Packer once said: "Members write in asking if this thing or that thing is against the Word of Wisdom. It's well known that tea, coffee, liquor, and tobacco are against it. *It has not been spelled out in more detail.* Rather, we teach the principle together with the promised blessing" ("The Word of Wisdom: The Principle and the Promises," *Ensign,* May 1996, 17; emphasis added).

You see, modern stripling warriors don't need to be told every little detail. The Lord expects us to figure some things out for ourselves. He has given us guidance, counsel, and modern prophets to advise us. He has provided the Holy Ghost to give us additional support. But in the end, there are some things he expects us to determine for ourselves.

Take a moment to consider how well you live up to the spirit of the Word of Wisdom. Are your habits healthy, uplifting, and refreshing? Or do they tend to hurt more than they help? Remember that the Word of

Wisdom was given to *bless* your life, to help you to be healthy and happy. Follow the counsel! Discover for yourself the Lord's great promises to those who do, finding wisdom and great treasures of knowledge.

WARRIOR WORKOUT TIPS

- If you've never broken the Word of Wisdom, vow that you never will. Let the Word of Wisdom be a strength in your life!
- If you have problems with any aspect of the Word of Wisdom, remember President Hinckley's counsel: "Stop now!" Don't let an earthly weakness damage or destroy your mind, spirit, or body. And if you ever feel tempted, remember his advice: "Stand your ground. . . . Do not throw away your future."
- Read D&C 89:18–21. Recognize and enjoy the blessings that come from obeying the commandments of our Heavenly Father. Remember that the purpose of the Word of Wisdom is not to *restrict* your life. It is to *bless* your life.

9

JOSEPH SMITH, ABINADI, AND YOU

Dealing with Adversity

Twelve-year-old Bobby Glazier's knuckles were white as he pulled on the tarp.

"Okay!" he yelled. "I'm ready!"

"All right," his father hollered back. "Hang on now!"

Mr. Glazier cinched the tarp down tight over the family boat, securing it with a bungee cord. He made a quick adjustment, and then yelled to Bobby on the other side of the boat.

"Now, pull it tight, Bob!"

Bobby clenched his teeth and pulled as hard as he could. He had the tarp almost where he wanted it when the fabric suddenly ripped. The bungee cord whipped across Bobby's face, slashing his right eye.

Mr. Glazier rushed Bobby to the hospital, where

doctors scrambled to save his eye. Eventually they tried surgery, while Bobby's family fasted and prayed. Bobby's father and bishop gave him a priesthood blessing. But after several days it became clear that nothing was going to work.

The surgeons had to remove Bobby's eye.

Throughout the ordeal, one person who kept a good attitude was Bobby.

"I didn't want to lose my eye," he told me. "No way! I cried and cried. But I knew I couldn't dwell on it. I knew I couldn't let it ruin my life. I knew I had to learn to deal with it and get on with my life.

"Besides," he said, "I knew that my Heavenly Father was watching over me. My dad gave me a blessing, and I knew then that I was going to be okay. I knew I wasn't going to get my eye back, but I knew I was going to be okay."

I thought that was an amazing attitude. Especially for someone so young.

At no other time is it harder to be valiant than when you're dealing with adversity. When serious problems come up they can distract you from deeper, more spiritual things. You might become obsessed wondering why certain things have to happen to *you*. You might wonder why *you* have to endure certain hardships, especially when you're working so hard to be valiant.

I have a young friend named Trevor who used to play on my eighth-grade basketball team. Two weeks before the league tournament began, he was in an accident and broke both arms.

Both arms!

We were both devastated (I think I was actually more traumatized than he was!), but Trevor's problems weren't over. Not long after his arms healed, his doctor discovered a lump behind his ear.

It was a tumor.

Trevor knew that he was in for some tough times. But—like Bobby—he refused to give up. He refused to let his problems get him down, and he even managed to keep his sense of humor. When he heard that—due to his treatments—he might lose his hair, he grinned and rubbed my head said: "It's okay, Coach! It just means I'm gonna look like you!"

The sad thing is that when things go wrong—when life becomes hard—many people *do* give up. But it's during the hard times that you need the support of your Heavenly Father more than ever. It's during adversity that you need to be especially close to him.

I used to teach a young woman named Hollie, whose mother passed away when Hollie was sixteen.

"Losing my mother was the hardest thing I've ever had to go through," Hollie told me. "I loved my mother. And I couldn't bear the thought of losing her."

Like Bobby, Hollie received a priesthood blessing. And she tried more than ever to become close to her Heavenly Father.

"I don't understand why it had to happen," she said. "But I know the Church is true and I trust Heavenly Father."

Remember that everyone has trials. And bad things happen. Even to good people. Remember Abinadi? One of the great messages from the story of Abinadi is that being good—even being a *prophet*—doesn't protect you from adversity (see Mosiah 17). We know about the stripling warriors because they were in the middle of a devastating war.

And don't forget Joseph Smith, who spent months in jail. Adding to his misery was the knowledge that while he was in jail, hundreds of faithful Saints were being driven from their homes by mobs, losing everything they had. Can you imagine the Prophet's pain? Can you understand why he cried out in Liberty Jail,

"O God, where art thou? . . . How long shall thy hand be stayed?" (D&C 121:1–2).

Have you ever wondered the same thing?

I have!

And the Lord's answer to Joseph Smith was the same as his answer to me. And it is the same to you: "My son [or daughter], peace be unto thy soul; thine adversity and thine afflictions shall be but a small moment; and then, if thou endure it well, God shall exalt thee on high" (D&C 121:7–8).

Remember that adversity is a part of life. But that's not the point. It's how you *act* and how you *perform* during the tough times that matters. So when hard times come into your life, remember these tips.

HAVE FAITH

When I was in college, I was once flying home from a long, cross-country trip in a small airplane. I had been in the air for several hours and I was tired, cramped, and anxious to get home. As I was flying over Salt Lake City, the air traffic controller called.

"Cessna Niner Zero Bravo," he said to me, "turn left ninety degrees and maintain altitude."

Why? I thought, as I acknowledged and turned my airplane. *Another couple of minutes and I'll be home. . . . Why do I have to do this now?*

I flew on my new heading for five or six minutes, and then, without any explanation, the controller was back.

"Niner Zero Bravo," he said in a flat, monotonous voice, "return to original course. Maintain altitude and have a good day."

"Yeah, right," I grumbled. But as I thought about it, I realized that I was aware only of myself and my little airplane. But the controller was sitting in front of a big screen watching dozens of planes—many of them filled with hundreds of people. He could see the big picture, and he understood things that I couldn't.

There might have been some in-flight emergency, for instance, and maybe he had to get me out of the way so that a faster plane could pass. I didn't know. And I didn't *need* to know.

I think that life is often like that. We see things through our own two eyes and are not aware of many of the other things going on around us. But our Heavenly Father sees the big picture. And sometimes he has to inconvenience us to bless someone else. Sometimes a particular hardship is necessary for our own progress.

It would be nice if we could know all the reasons why things have to happen. But it's more important that we have faith in our Heavenly Father. It's important that we trust him enough to know that he has everything under control and that everything is going to be okay. It's important that we trust him enough to believe that our hardships will give us experience and, in the end, be for our good (see D&C 122:7).

PRAY

Remember that no matter what you're going through, your Heavenly Father knows exactly how you feel. He knows what you're going through. By sharing your problems with him, you invite the comfort and blessings of the one Being who really understands.

Remember when Joseph Smith went into the grove to pray? He was suddenly overcome by a spirit of blackness that fought to overcome him.

"I was seized upon by some power which entirely overcame me," he said, "and had such an astonishing influence over me as to bind my tongue so that I could not speak. Thick darkness gathered around me, and it seemed to be for a time as if I were doomed to sudden destruction" (Joseph Smith–History 1:15).

So what did Joseph do? When he was so nearly overcome with blackness and darkness that he thought he was about to die, how did he react?

He began to pray *even harder!*

What a wonderful example this is. When adversity threatens to pull *you* down, follow the prophet's example. Work harder! Pray harder! Become even more valiant!

Concentrate on Solutions

When things go wrong, it's easy to begin asking questions like, "Why is this happening to me?"

But wondering *why* won't help you to solve anything. It'll only make you miserable and keep you from getting any sleep. More important, it will keep you from finding solutions.

So when things go wrong, concentrate on solutions. Ask yourself, "What am I going to *do* about this?" Then spend your energy coming up with answers.

Elder LeGrand Richards once shared this poem:

For every worry under the sun,
There is a remedy, or there is none;
If there be one, hurry and find it,
If there be none, never mind it.

(*Church News,* March 31, 1974, 4)

As you search for solutions, don't hesitate to ask for help. Talk with your parents, teachers, friends, or counselors. Visit with your bishop. Ask for a priesthood blessing.

Channel Your Feelings in Positive Directions

You know how you feel when you're having a bad day? And you know how it feels when someone notices your pain and does something nice for you? You know how it feels if someone gives you a hug? Or a word of encouragement?

Then give one to someone else! Look around for people who could use a pat on the back and give it to them. Write a note and leave it in their notebook. Hide a candy bar in their locker. Take the time to lift a life. You'll not only make someone else feel better, but by focusing your energy in a positive direction *you'll* feel better, too.

I know a young woman named Kelsie whose older brother, Trent, was going through a rebellious stage. He began skipping classes at school and he often snuck out of church. His parents wondered if he might be smoking or drinking.

Life at home became a nightmare. There were fights and arguments whenever Trent was around. Instead of being a refuge where she could relax from the pressures of her own day, Kelsie's home became oppressive and miserable. Whenever Trent was home Kelsie felt like bursting out and running away.

But instead, she took a different approach. Whenever things started getting tense, she took her little brother and sister and drove them to the park.

"I knew that if things seemed bad to me, they had to be worse for Andy and Jenny," she said. "They didn't understand what was going on. So I decided to do everything I could to make them feel better."

It was many months before Kelsie's home became somewhat normal again. But besides helping Andy and Jenny, she gave her parents one less thing to worry about. She was a key in helping her family become strong again.

Remember that everyone has trials. Everyone has problems at some time or another. When your turn comes, don't let your trials get you down. Instead, become even closer to your Heavenly Father. Draw on his strength to help you through.

It'll be hard. But be assured that as you strive to work through your problems, your Heavenly Father will be with you. And know "that all these things shall give thee experience, and shall be for thy good" (D&C 122:7).

Warrior Workout Tips

- When trials come into your life, don't waste time asking, "Why me?" Instead, ask questions such as, "What should I do now?" or "What does the Lord want me to learn from this?"

- Remember to pray. Don't pray that your problems will simply go away, but pray for the strength, help, and guidance to *endure*. Pray for the ability to work through your challenges.

- Count your blessings. Though you might face devastating hardships, there are certain to be blessings in your life, too. Be grateful for them! Focus on the blessings you have rather than the trials you face.

- Concentrate on solutions. Don't waste time worrying that you have problems. Instead, put your energy to work finding solutions to them.

10

BECOMING LIKE MORONI

Becoming a Stripling Warrior

The ski lodge was dark and quiet as I pushed the last pine log into the fireplace. The snapping flames made the only sounds as I stepped back and surveyed the lodge. It was past midnight, and almost everyone else had long since gone to bed.

My eighteen-year-old friend Jeff was reading his Book of Mormon by the light of the fire as I warmed my hands over the crackling flames.

"Wow," Jeff said softly.

"Wow, what?" I asked.

Jeff looked up. "Oh, I was just reading about Captain Moroni," he said. He shook his head in admiration. "He was awesome, wasn't he?"

"Yeah," I said. "He really was."

Jeff was staring into the fire now, his eyes full of

wonder. "Wouldn't it be awesome," he asked, "if you could be like Moroni?"

"Yes," I said. "It would."

That thought stayed with me long after I went to bed that night. Wouldn't it be awesome if you *could* be like Moroni? Or Nephi? Or Ammon? Or Helaman's stripling warriors?

Wouldn't it be awesome if you could be like President Monson?

You can, you know!

You can be valiant in whatever calling the Lord has given you. You can be valiant in the Church. You can be valiant in magnifying your priesthood calling. You can be valiant in serving your Young Women's class. You can be a valiant deacon, a valiant Laurel, or a valiant missionary. You can be valiant in your family. You can be valiant in paying your tithing, obeying the Word of Wisdom, or praying.

You can start today, setting your goals and standards high, and working to meet them. You can be a latter-day stripling warrior who is "true . . . in whatsoever thing [you are] entrusted" (Alma 53:20).

When I was in high school I had a recreation class. My teacher was a man named Al, who was one of my personal heroes. Besides being an awesome teacher, Al knew how to bring out the best in me. He was constantly pushing me, challenging me, and guiding me toward new and exciting goals.

One afternoon we were rappelling off cliffs in a nearby canyon. I was belaying my friend Sam as he bounced down the rocks, and Al was watching me. He watched as I tied my knots, braced myself against the rocks, called out my commands, and let the rope slide through my gloved hands.

After Sam landed safely at the bottom of the cliff, Al walked over and tapped me on the shoulder.

"Good job, Shane," he said. "You're a natural. I'd trust you with my life."

That was one of the single most incredible moments of my life. I wouldn't have felt any more invincible if I'd just heard that I'd been picked to be the starting pitcher in the World Series or trumpet soloist for the London Philharmonic. Al put me on cloud nine. His simple praise charged and energized me, and I knew what it would feel like to be Batman, Spiderman, and Superman all rolled into one.

I remember another time when my bishop came over and sat beside me before priesthood meeting. He mentioned something I'd done recently—something I didn't think he even knew about—and said: "I want you to know how much I appreciate you. I hope my boys grow up to be just like you."

I felt that incredible sensation all over again. It was an awesome experience. I felt so phenomenal that if the bishop had then asked me to move a mountain, build a temple, or spend the next fifty years on a mission, I would have jumped right up and done it!

As wonderful as those experiences were, though, there's one thing I know that would be immeasurably better. And that would be to one day stand in front of my Heavenly Father, have him take me in his arms, and say, "Well done, thou good and faithful servant."

Wouldn't that be incredible?

It could happen!

And it could happen to *you!*

The question is, are you fulfilling the mission you were sent here for? Are you getting the job done? Are you doing everything your Heavenly Father expects of you?

Or are you sitting by while someone else does the work that *you* are here to do?

Don't let that happen!

Remember that you are here at this time and this place for a special reason. Your Father in Heaven saved *you* for a great purpose. He has given *you* an important mission, and he needs *you* to get it done.

Winston Churchill once said: "To every man there comes . . . that special moment when he is figuratively tapped on the shoulder and offered the chance to do a special thing unique to him and fitted to his talent. What a tragedy if that moment finds him unprepared or unqualified for the work which would be his finest hour" (quoted by Elder Jeffrey R. Holland, "Sanctify Yourselves," *Ensign,* Nov. 2000, 38).

Remember that whatever your Heavenly Father has planned for you, no one else will ever be able to do it exactly the way that you can. No one else has exactly the same skills, talents, and abilities that you do. If you are not ready—or worthy—to do the job when the time comes, it might not get done as well. It might not even get done at all.

I have a friend named Matt who recently returned from his mission. He told me that one evening he met with a family who had heard the discussions many times and from several different missionaries.

"But from the first moment I met them I felt

something change," Matt said. "I knew they were feeling the witness of the Holy Ghost, and I challenged them to be baptized. And they were."

You see, there was something about Matt that touched the family in a way that no one had ever done before. They were a family waiting for the gospel. But Matt was able to reach them in a way that no one else was able to.

Like Matt, you will be able to reach some people better than anyone else. There are things that need to be done that you will be able to do better than anyone else.

Several years ago, President Spencer W. Kimball was scheduled for a delicate heart operation. Presidents Harold B. Lee and N. Eldon Tanner gave a blessing to the surgeon, Dr. Russell M. Nelson, promising him "that the operation would be performed without error, that all would go well and that . . . [he] had been raised up by the Lord to perform [that] operation" ("News of the Church," *Ensign,* May 1984, 87).

Be assured that the Lord is raising *you* up for important work, too. Your personal mission may not be as dramatic as performing heart surgery on a prophet. But in the eyes of your Heavenly Father, it will certainly be important.

"Perhaps you have something to give that is as simple as love," said Bishop H. Burke Peterson, "or dedication, or hard work, or anything else that may be missing in someone's life. Try it. Share it. You'll never know what it may do for another" ("Your Life Has a Purpose," *New Era,* May 1979, 4).

Remember the words of the song:

> *I'll go where you want me to go, dear Lord,*
> *Over mountain or plain or sea;*
> *I'll say what you want me to say, dear Lord;*
> *I'll be what you want me to be.*
>   (*Hymns,* 1985, no. 270)

My young friends, we have work to do. *You* have work to do. And it's time to get started. Don't waste another minute. Start now and begin preparing yourself so that when the Lord needs you, you'll be ready.

Be as valiant as Moroni was! Be as valiant as Nephi and Ammon and the two thousand stripling warriors. Live your life so that when someone, someday, writes about your generation he can say, "They were all young men and young women, and they were *exceedingly* valiant!"

WARRIOR WORKOUT TIPS

- Be valiant! Begin every day determined to follow the example of Jesus and be the best person you can be.
- Take advantage of your youth. As a young person you have tremendous energy and enthusiasm. Use your gifts to be an example for good in the lives of your friends and family!
- Take a moment and think of some specific things you can do to become even more valiant. Commit to doing them. Start now!
- Remember that little acts are often as important as big ones. Look for little ways to bless the lives of others. Look for people you can help with a smile or a helping hand.
- Now . . . get up! Get out! And get to work!